100 STORIES
That Have Served Me Well

100 STORIES
That Have Served Me Well

LAWRENCE A. WIEN

Foreword by Abram L. Sachar

Richardson & Steirman
1984

Type and case design: Mr. Galen Bushey
Jacket design: Mr. David Gatti
Composition: Paragraphics, New York, NY

Foreword

Chancellor Abram L. Sachar
Brandeis University

Besides his many talents as an extraordinarily resourceful counselor at law and as a perceptive philanthropist, Larry Wien has been one of the great raconteurs for almost three generations. Some of his stories, to be sure, can only be told to a very special audience, who won't be able to restrain a belly laugh, and then, *sotto voce*. Of course, occasionally, Larry may be scolded for corrupting priests, nuns, tax accountants and deans, and thus eschew their professional austerity.

But Larry tells his stories not only to entertain. His own laugh is not only the loudest and most sustained but it's infectious. Many of these stories carry a unique relevance. When he is introduced at an affair with too many flattering adjectives, he is a master in the self-deprecating retort. When a committee goes on too tediously and reaches the point of repetitiveness, he comes up with a story that brings his group back to relevant reality. And even a locker room anecdote, which would bring a blush to a burlesque queen, usually carries a special prod in the punch line that breaks down all inhibitions. Many of his friends have heard him repeat stories endlessly but they listen attentively, if only to share the delight of Larry's own contagious enjoyment.

There are those who believe that Larry will stop telling some of these stories as the years pass and his views about life move into "the sere and yellow." I don't anticipate this, for Larry will never grow old.

Author's Introduction

Through the years I have been obliged to do a considerable amount of public speaking. I have found that my audiences stay awake more easily if I open my address with a good story. In addition, the telling of an enjoyable story can make one very popular in social groups, and this is something we all like.

To be a successful storyteller, you really don't need more than 100 stories. You will find that as you grow older, you will be meeting new audiences of younger people. They haven't heard your stories before.

Even more importantly, your friends and contemporaries grow older with you, they lose their memories and, you can tell them the same stories over and over again. I recommend the following 100 to you—and at $8.95 for the book, you are paying less than 9¢ a story.

Have fun.

100 STORIES

Dedication

To Mae,
who has made it possible for me to laugh
for so many years.

100 STORIES

Section I
The stories in the first group are general in character and can be told to anyone, anywhere.

1

When God was handing out the attributes of the different animals he said to Man—"I'm going to give you 20 years of sex life." And Man said, "All right."

Then God turned to the Monkey, and he said, I'm going to give you 20 years of sex life." The Monkey said, "Look, God, I'm only a small animal and I get tired. Ten years are enough for me." And God said, "All right." And Man raised his hand and said, "God, can I have the Monkey's extra ten years of sex life?" And God said, "All right."

Then God turned to the Jackass and He said, "You're a strong animal and I'll give you 20 years of sex life." And the Jackass said, "God. They work me like a dog. I get home exhausted. Ten years are enough for me." And God said, "All right." And again Man raised his hand and said "God. Can I have the Jackass's extra ten years of sex life?" And God said, "All right."

And then God turned to the Lion and said, "You're the king of the beasts. I'm going to give you 30 years of sex life." And the Lion said, "Look, God. You know I'm the king of the beasts and I know it. But the elephants, and the rhinoceros and the hippopotamuses, they don't know it, and they beat the hell out of me. I get home bloody and bedraggled and 10 years are enough for me." And God said, "All right." And for the third time, Man raised his hand, and said "Can I have the Lion's 20 extra years of sex life?" And God said, "All right."

And that's why it is that Man has 20 years of sex life, 10 years of monkeying around, 10 years of making a jackass of himself, and 20 years of lyin' about it.

2

The wife said to her husband, "You have trouble with your Rolls-Royce."

"What's that?"

"Your Rolls-Royce has water in the carburetor."

"Water in the carburetor? That's ridiculous."

"I tell you your car has water in the carburetor."

"You don't even know what a carburetor is. Where is the car?"

"In the swimming pool."

3

They pulled the man out of the water in Miami Beach, laid him down on the sand at the water's edge and started to work on him. They pressed on his chest and green water came out of his mouth. They pressed on his chest and green water came out of his mouth. This went on for 15 minutes—pressing on his chest and green water coming out of his mouth.

A little Jewish bystander suddenly said, "Podden me. I'm not a doctor, not a scientist, not even an engineer but what you're doing is wrong."

"What do you mean?"

"If you don't take his behind out of the water, you'll pump out the whole ocean."

4

The aging golfer said, "I'm 75 and I can drive the ball almost as far as I ever did, but I can't see where it goes. My eyesight is bad." His friend said, "I'm 85 and I can't drive the ball far, but I've got excellent eyesight—I've got 20/20 vision. Let's play together tomorrow—you drive it and I'll watch it." They did and the first golfer drove the ball. "Did you see it?" "Yep." "Did you follow it?" "Yep." "Where is it?" "I forget."

5

He was old and retired. He and his young wife took many trips. On one tour they arrived at Calcutta. As they moved into their suite in the hotel, she said, "I'd love to see a Hindu temple." He said, "I'm tired. You go and see the Hindu temple and then tell me about it. I'm going to lie down."

She went to a Hindu temple where there were a lot of snakecharmers in the courtyard, who played on their flutes and the snakes came weaving up out of their baskets. There was one snakecharmer, however, who was different. He blew on his flute and the snake came up from the basket, but instead of weaving, it came straight up and stood erect and stiff. She said, "That's a remarkable flute you have there." The snakecharmer said, "You haven't seen anything yet, Madam." And he blew on his flute again, and from the adjacent basket an ordinary piece of string came shooting up out of the basket and stood firm, and erect, and stiff. Well, she started negotiations and bought the flute for $2,000.

She came back to the suite in the hotel, and sure enough her husband was lying in bed, with the covers up to his neck. "Darling, I got a most unusual flute, and I'd like you to listen to it." He said nothing. "It really has a lovely tone and I'd love to have you listen to it." Again he said nothing. "Just listen to it, darling," she said, and she began to blow into the flute.

As she blew, the bedclothes started to rise from her husband's bed. She kept blowing and the bedclothes kept going higher and higher.

Suddenly he said, "Becky—look what happened to the string on my pajamas!"

6

The two little elderly men were walking along Collins Avenue in Miami Beach. Said one, "I'm sick of this retirement business. I've got nothing to do, and I hate it."

His friend said "What you should have is a 'obby."

"You got a 'obby?"

"Yup."

"What is it?"

"I raise bees."

"You raise bees. What have you got? A farm?"

"No, I live in an apartment and I raise the bees there."

"But how can you? They'll sting you and everybody."

"No they don't."

"Why not?"

"I keep them in a closet."

"But you open the door and they come out, they'll sting everybody."

"No they don't."

"Why not?"

"Because I keep them in a box in the closet."

"In a box? But you've got to have airholes in the box and they'll fly out through the airholes and sting everybody."

"I don't have airholes in the box."

"No airholes? Then they'll die."

"So let 'em die. It's only a 'obby."

7

The elderly husband said to his wife—"I had the strangest experience last night. During the night I had to go to the bathroom. When I got there, the light went on itself, before I could touch the switch. And when I left, the light went off before I touched the switch." She said, "Sam, you went to the refrigerator again."

8

The little widow, on the lower East Side, went into a photography shop, which advertised that they restored old photographs. She produced an old photo and said, "This is my husband. He was such a handsome man. Can you restore this picture?"

"Yes, Madam, we can."

"You know, he worked so hard and he was so busy. You see his nose—it's too big—he always meant to have it operated on, but he never had the time. Maybe, when you restore the picture, you can shorten the nose?"

"Yes, Madam, we can do that."

"That's fine. And you notice, he has a hat on. He had such beautiful hair. Maybe, when you restore the picture, you can take his hat off?"

"Yes, Madam, we can do that."

The little lady was just leaving when the clerk-proprietor said, "Madam—your husband—did he part his hair on the left side or the right side?"

"Silly," she said, "You'll take off the hat, you'll see."

9

The hard-working husband came home and said to his wife, "I've had a terrible day at the office and I'm exhausted. I don't want to hear any problems. Talk to me, but tell me only good news. What's today's good news?"

"Good news," said the wife. "You know you have six children?"

"Yes."

"Well, the good news is that five of them did not break their arms today."

10

An Italian immigrant was applying for citizenship. He was asked, "What is the capital of the United States?"
He proudly answered, "Washington, D.C."
"Right—and what does D.C. stand for?"
"Dat'sa easy—D.C. is De Capital."

11

The local politician was cautious. He never offended anyone by taking a definite position. He was criticized but always saw at least two sides to every dispute—and appeared to favor both.

Finally, a heckler said, "I've been trying to get you to give a clear and definite answer—and I have a question which compels you to take a definite position. What is your favorite color?"

The politician replied—"Plaid."

12

Three nuns died and went to Heaven. St. Peter's representative said, "You were very good girls on earth and you can be anyone you wish up here."

The first said, "I want to be Marilyn Monroe." The representative said, "O.K."

The second said, "I want to be Jean Harlow."

"And so you are," said St. Pete's rep.

The third said, "I want to be Sarah Pippelini."

The rep said, "O.K., but—wait a minute. Who is Sarah Pippelini?"

"You never heard of Sarah Pippelini?"

"No."

"Do you get the New York Times up here?"

"We do."

"Can you get me yesterday's New York Times?"

"Yes." And after a few minutes he returned and said, "Here it is."

"There," said the third nun, "read that—Sarah Pippelini laid by 10,000 Arabs."

"You're reading that wrong. It's Sahara Pipeline laid by 10,000 Arabs."

13

The husband and wife were asleep. Suddenly she nudged him. "I hear a noise. I think there's a burglar downstairs." They listened and heard nothing.

He said "Go to sleep. It's your imagination."

A little later she said, "I hear someone downstairs again. It must be a burglar. Go down and see."

Grumbling, he does. He turns on the lights, and as he is descending the stairs he sees a man in their living room.

"Are you a burglar?" he says.

"No. I'm a rapist."

"Dorothy," he calls, "it's for you."

14

A representative of a pharmaceutical company, called Chesebrough-Pond's, was making a survey and asked a housewife if she used the products of his company.

"Oh, yes," she said, "we use all kinds of cheese."

"But we don't make cheese, Madam; we make drug products, like petroleum jelly. Do you use petroleum jelly?"

"Oh, yes."

"Really. Will you please forgive me if I ask a rather personal question, for our survey? Do you use petroleum jelly in connection with sex?"

"Oh, yes."

"How?"

"When my husband and I have sex, we put it on the handle of the door to our bedroom, so the children can't come in."

15

The tired-looking little man was sitting on a bench in Central Park. A powerful-looking giant of a man sat down beside him, and after a few moments said, "I'm from Texas, and in Texas we can do anything." Throwing out his chest, he said, "Look at this. Can you make a chest like that?"

"No," said the little man.

"And look at the muscle on my right arm. Can you make a muscle like that?"

"No," said the little man.

"And feel that thigh muscle. Can you make a muscle like that?"

"No," said the little man.

"I don't think you softies can do anything I can't do. Can you do anything I can't do?", said the big Texan.

When you tell the story, stand up at this point, pull down the zipper on your fly. Then pull out your shirt-tail and say, "Can you make a shirt like this for $12 a dozen?"

16

Mrs. Ginsberg was demonstrating her knowledge of art, as she walked with her friends and a guide at the Metropolitan Museum.

"That's a Gauguin, isn't it?" The guide acknowledged that it was.

"And that's a Renoir. Right?"

"Yes, it is," said the guide.

"And that's a Picasso. Right?"

"No, Madam, that's a mirror."

17

Speakers at various dinners and similar functions are sometimes introduced with excessive praise. There are a few "deflating" stories, which clearly indicate that the speaker does not believe the description by the person introducing him. The following story is one of the best.

After speaking at a Brandeis University function, I was on a receiving line with the President of the University and the President of the Women's Committee. We were introduced to people as they passed, and a youngster of 14 or 15 was in the line. He was introduced to me and said, "Mr. Wien, you spoke too long." He passed along, came around to the end of the line and when he again arrived before me said, "And Mr. Wien, you spoke too loud." He came around a third time and said, "And Mr. Wien, you didn't say anything worth listening to."

The lady next to me said, "Mr. Wien, don't let that silly kid upset you. All he does is repeat what everybody else says."

18

Mr. O'Brien was proud of his ancestry. He spent a lot of money to obtain a genealogical table. Unfortunately, family research showed that one of his forebears had been found guilty of murder and was executed in the electric chair. With the aid of his advisor, he had this ancestor join the listed academicians and jurists by describing him as having "occupied a chair in applied electricity," and "he died in harness."

19

A young married couple were having difficulty in making a baby. They enjoyed the effort over several years, then finally consulted a doctor who examined each of them separately. He assured each one that there was no physical reason which prevented them from having children. The husband had a separate conference with the doctor and he asked what he could possibly do to solve the problem. The doctor stated that he thought the difficulty lay in the fact that his wife was trying too hard and was tense all the time. He suggested that what the husband should do was try to have relations with his wife when she didn't expect him and therefore did not have an opportunity to tense up.

He said, "You try to do this and come back in three months and tell me what happened."

The husband went away and returned three months later. The doctor asked him whether he had followed his advice.

The husband said, "I certainly did."

The doctor said, "What happened?"

"Well," he said, "one day when she least expected it, I came from behind her and I put it to her right there and then and she was absolutely surprised."

The doctor said, "That's wonderful. And then what happened?"

The husband said, "We were kicked out of Schrafft's."

20

A second deflation story: I was introduced at a fund-raising dinner where I was the principal speaker and the introduction was very extravagant, but I was impressed by it. When I got home, as I slowly undressed in front of a full-length mirror, I asked my wife, "How many really great men do you think there are alive today?"

She answered, "One less than you think."

21

Father Murphy was assigned by his Bishop to a parish in Alaska. After he had been there for two years, the Bishop decided that he should visit Father Murphy and see how he was getting along. When he arrived, he found Father Murphy comfortably established in a two-room igloo, and he seemed to be enjoying himself. The Bishop asked Father Murphy how he was getting along. Father Murphy said, "Between my Rosary and my martinis, I get along very well."

"By the way, Bishop," he said, "would you like a martini?"

The Bishop said, "Yes, I would like a martini."

Father Murphy said, "Rosary, bring in two martinis."

22

The last of the deflating stories: I was walking along with my wife. We came to a scale. I got on the scale and a card came out containing my weight and some other material. I said to my wife, "You're younger than I am and I don't have my glasses with me. Read the card. What does it say?" She read, "It says you are brilliant, you are handsome, you're a genius, you are courteous," and, she said, "You are most attractive to women—and it has your weight wrong also."

23

The Jewish emigre from Russia came to Vienna, which was the usual stopping-point for people on the way from Russia to other countries. The agent in the office for emigrants asked him what country he'd like to go to.

The emigre said, "Well, you tell me what countries you've got?"

The officer said, "I can give you Israel?"

He said, "No, not Israel...I don't speak Hebrew and there are too many Jewish people there. I'd like to be in a more mixed group."

The officer said, "I can give you Australia?"

"Oh," the emigre said, "Australia is much too far away. I don't think I'd like to be there. There are no Jews there to speak of."

"I can give you Argentina?"

"Oh, Argentina is too far away and they speak a foreign language."

"I can give you the United States?"

He said, "Well, the United States might be all right, but I have so many relatives there, I'd rather not go there."

Finally, the agent said, "Look, here's a map of the world. Look at it and see what countries you might like to go to." He went away for about ten minutes and he came back and said to the emigre, "Have you picked a country?"

"No," he said. "Any other countries?"

"No," the agent said, "they're all on the map."

The emigre said, "Can you give me another map?"

24

A test was being given to young men and women who were becoming policemen in New York City and the young Irish police recruit had finished all of the questions, except for one. The question was, "What are rabies, and what can you do about it?"

The young man was not familiar with rabies. He didn't have much to do with dogs. There aren't so many people who have dogs in New York City. After puzzling for a while, he finally wrote, "Rabies are Jewish priests, and there is nothing you can do about it."

25

A man decided he wanted a divorce after ten years of marriage. This was the second marriage for both him and his wife. They came before the judge and he told the judge that he wanted a divorce. His wife said, "Never. I won't give him a divorce, unless he can leave me exactly as he found me."

The judge said, "Well, my dear woman, after ten years you can't expect everything to be exactly the same."

She said, "Why not? He found me a widow and I want he should leave me a widow."

26

A famous physician in England was leading a group of students through a hospital and was commenting on the diseases of the patients they examined. He would take each patient's chart and describe and interpret the symptoms. Then he would diagnose the illness.

The first one—he described the symptoms and said, "PN", which means pneumonia. The second one—he described the symptoms and said, "TB"—which was tuberculosis. The third one—he described the symptoms and he said, "G-O-K." The fourth one—he described the symptoms and said, "AP"—angina pectoris. The fifth one—he described the symptoms and said, "MAL"—malaria. The sixth one—he described the symptoms and said, "G-O-K." This went on with quite a few G-O-Ks. Finally, one of the students said to him, "Doctor, we understand what you say about most of these ailments, but what is G-O-K? What ailment is G-O-K?" The physician said, "G-O-K means, 'God only knows'."

27

I say that my first grandchild, a little girl, was a mathe-matical wizard. When she was in first grade, she came home and told her father that she had won the arithmetic prize in her class. Her father asked, "What happened? That was wonderful!"

"Well," she said, "The teacher asked us what was six times seven and I said 35 and I was closer than everyone else in the class."

28

A mother was having trouble with her son. He was addicted to the use of dirty language. He came down to breakfast one day and after she had asked what he would have, he said, "Give me some of those goddamned cornflakes."

She was provoked and slapped him. She turned to her husband and said, "And what will you have?"

He said, "I don't know, but you can bet your ass that it won't be cornflakes."

29

This is really the description of a cartoon. The cartoon shows a girl leaping out of bed, with a man lying in bed, and underneath is the line, "What do you mean, you want a mulligan?"

30

A man of 83 went to his doctor and said, "Doctor, I want you to lower my sex drive."

The doctor said, "At 83? That's ridiculous, it's all in your head."

The patient said, "That's just it, doctor. I want you to lower my sex drive."

31

Two residents of a home for the aged were sitting in rocking chairs and talking. The first one said, "Jake, you know, you're married and you have your wife. I'm a widower and I'm alone. Tell me, do you still do anything?" Jake said, "I certainly do. Once a month, like clockwork."

They rocked a while and the first one said, "Jake, I don't believe you." He said, "If you do it twice a year, that's not bad." Jake said, "All right, not once a month, but twice a year—every winter, every summer, like clockwork."

They rocked a while and the first one said, "In the summer it's hot and it's debilitating. Jake, I don't believe you do it in the summer." Jake said, "All right, not in the summer, but every winter, like clockwork."

They rocked a little longer and the first one said, "Jake every winter? How about this winter?" Jake said, "You call this a winter?"

32

A married couple was revisiting the hotel at which they had stayed 45 years before, on their honeymoon. As they lay in bed, the wife said, "You know, Tom, this is very different from the way it was 45 years ago. Then you bit my cheek, you bit my ear, you bit my breasts..." He started to run out of the bed and she said, "Where are you going?" He said, "I'm going to get my teeth."

33

A man came to an airline counter and wanted to get two tickets to Pittsburgh. The girl behind the counter had on a low-cut blouse and had the most beautiful bust development he had ever seen. It was so beautiful, that the man's attention was drawn to it and he looked and looked and stared, and she became more and more embarrassed. Finally, she said to him, "You are embarrassing me terribly. Please stop looking at me that way and tell me what you want."

He said, "Oh, I apologize. All I want is two pickets to Tittsburgh."

34

There is a chap outside my office building who sells shoelaces at 25 cents a pair. I don't use shoelaces. I wear slip-on shoes. I find them more comfortable. But he is a poor man, and needs a little help, and every time I pass him I buy a pair of shoelaces for 25 cents, but I don't take the shoelaces. The other day he stopped me and said, "Mr. Wien, I would like to tell you something."

I said, "You want to ask me why I never take the shoelaces."

"No," he said, "it's not that. I just wanted to tell you that, because of inflation, the price of shoelaces is now 50 cents a pair."

35

A farmer bought a special rooster. He figured the rooster would service his hens well. The rooster did, but the rooster wasn't satisfied with the hens alone and he saw some ducks, so he flew out of the yard, reached the ducks, and he serviced the ducks the same way.

The farmer said to the rooster, "Look, I got you to service only the chickens—the hens." He said, "If you're going to run around the way you do, you're going to kill yourself through overexertion."

Despite that, a couple of days later, the rooster flew out of the yard and found some geese and he proceeded to service all of them.

When the farmer found out, he got angrier and angrier and he said to the rooster, "I told you, you're going to kill yourself. Now stop it. Get back in that goddamned cage. I want you to service only the hens."

But despite the repeated admonitions by the farmer, the rooster flew out of the pen again and was found by the farmer, lying in the road, dead.

The farmer got angry. He said "You bastard, what happened was exactly what I told you would happen, you killed yourself through overexertion."

Over the rooster, buzzards were circling and were getting closer and closer. The rooster opened one eye, looked up at the farmer and said, "If you want to screw a buzzard, you got to play their game."

36

This is the story of a man who was despondent and melancholy. He was taken by his family to every psychologist, psychoanalyst and psychiatrist in the United States, without any success. Finally, the last psychiatrist said to him, "Look, there is only one man in the world who may possibly be helpful to you. He is a Doctor Finkelhof, who has a clinic in Berne, Switzerland, and if you can arrange to get an appointment at his clinic, he will examine you. If anybody can help you, he will."

Well, through influence, they succeeded in getting an appointment at Doctor Finkelhof's clinic and in due time he arrived at his appointment there. He met Doctor Finkelhof who said, "My frand, ve vill gif you ze most gomplete eggsamination anyvun has efer had, und ven ve are zrough mit ze eggsamination, ve vill know vat's vat." ►

And so they had the examination, which took almost a week, and they had a final conference. Doctor Finkelhof said, "You haf had ze eggsamination vat I told you." He said, "Und to understand your gundition, you must know the hooman body." He said, "The hooman body has got all zrough it narves. Narves yust like electric vires. For every part of your body, you got there narves. You got an elbow narve. In ze back, you haf the asshole narve. You got a finger narve. Up by the eye there, you got a optic narve." He said, "You got a belly narve— every place in your body, like electric vires, you got narves." He said, "Und yust like electric vires, zum- times the narves get crossed. Und your trouble, my frand, is dot your optic narve got crossed mit your ass- hole narve, und dot's vy you got such a shitty outlook on life."

37

This is the story of God, who called Moses and said, "Look, Mo, I got a lot of Hebrews who are being exploited in Egypt, and I want to give them a break." He said, "I'm going to move them to a new land with lots of milk and honey."

He said, "I want you to lead the Hebrews out of Egypt. All you have to do is head for the Red Sea and I'll give you further instructions later."

Moses said, "O.K., God."

He gathered the Hebrews together and he started for the Red Sea. And after a while, he noticed that behind him, the Egyptians had gathered together and were following them. They were getting closer. He got to the Red Sea and he called God. ▶

"God," he said, "I got a problem."

He said, "I'm at the Red Sea and the Egyptians are getting closer and closer. What am I supposed to do?"

God said, "Listen, Mo, I'm taking care of this. I'm going to bring down a wind so strong it's going to blow the Red Sea in half and there will be an alley that you and the Hebrews are going to march through and the Egyptians are going to follow you, and after you get through and the Egyptians are in the middle of the Red Sea, I'm going to take away the winds, and they are all going to be drowned."

Moses said, "God, that's a wonderful idea. You're doing one hell of a job up there. I think you're terrific."

God said, "Thanks, Mo, but I've got one problem."

Moses said, "What's that?"

God said, "In order for me to carry out this plan, I have to first get the approval of the Environmental Protection Agency."

38

A note was left by President Reagan for Vice President Bush. As you undoubtedly know, the President has a few problems. The note said, "Dear George: I'm going on vacation. Why don't you do me a favor? While I'm away, solve something."

39

This is the story of a lawsuit between two families who hated each other, something like the Hatfields and McCoys'. In any event, the trial was held. They called each other every kind of name. It became more and more unpleasant. The entire atmosphere in the courtroom was very, very unpleasant. But the case was finally finished, the testimony was concluded, the judge charged the jury, and the jury went out.

It came back after a while, and the judge said to the foreman of the jury, "Has the jury reached a decision?"

The foreman said, "It has."

The judge said, "What is the decision of the jury?"

The foreman said, "The jury has decided not to get involved in this case."

40

Enrico Fermi led the research that resulted in the Atom Bomb. The research was done in Oak Ridge, Tennessee. The Manhattan Project was conducted in a building that had an imposing flight of steps at the entrance. One day, a friend met Fermi as he was coming down the staircase. After they spoke for a while and they were about to part, Fermi said to his friend, "Tell me, when I met you was I going up the steps or coming down the steps?"

His friend said, "You were coming down the steps." "Oh," he said, "then I've already had my lunch."

41

Two men met. One fellow slapped the other on the back and said, "Jake Cohen, it's a pleasure to see you. Why, I haven't seen you or spoken with you ever since we lived together down on the Lower East Side."

The other man said, "I remember that, but my name is not Jake Cohen."

"Well," the other said, "What is it?"

He said, "My name is now C. R. Eldredge."

"C. R. Eldredge? That's a very impressive name. Where did you ever get that name?"

Jake Cohen said, "You know how we used to live on Eldredge Street? I took the name Eldredge from the street."

His friend said, "That's wonderful, but tell me, what is C. R.?"

The other said, "It's obvious—'Corner Rivington.'"

42

There was a lion featured in the circus and he was handled by a lion tamer who got sick and died as they were approaching an important town. The owner of the circus advertised for people who could handle the lion, and there were several applicants. One was a woman and two were men. One was a young chap, but one was an older man. The woman went first. She got into the cage with the lion. She took off her clothes and the lion nuzzled up against her and was very easy to handle. When she came out, the owner said to the two men, "Do you think you can compete with that?"

The old man said, "I can certainly do better."

The owner said, "You mean that after you saw what just happened there?"

The man said, "You're damn right. Just get that crazy lion out of the cage, and I'll show you."

43

A mountainclimber lost his footing and was sliding down the mountain. He grabbed hold of a small branch that was sticking out of the rocks, and he hung on with one arm, for dear life. He started to pray, and he said, "Oh, God, please help me, help me. God, I need help," and he looked up as he prayed, and all of a sudden, a voice came from on high and said,

"I am the Lord your God. What is it?"

And the man said, "Oh, God, please, I'm stuck here and I'm going to die if I don't get some help. Please, God, help me."

God said, "Do you believe in me?"

The man said, "I certainly do, God. I believe in you. I do believe."

God said, "Do you have complete faith in me?"

The man said, "Yes, I have complete faith in you, God."

God said, "Then let go of the bush."

After a moment, the man said, "Tell me, God, is there anybody else up there?"

44

There was a priest who had a lot of spare time, not having any particular family problems, and he became an expert on puzzles and riddles. He had a friend who was a Rabbi, and he said to the Rabbi:

"Rabbi, I'll tell you, you know I'm an expert on puzzles. I think we're going to have some fun. I'll tell you what. You ask me a riddle or a puzzle and if I can't answer your riddle, I'll give you $10. I'll ask you a riddle and if you can't answer it, all you have to do is give me $1."

The Rabbi said, "Fine."

The priest said, "All right, Rabbi, what is the first riddle?"

The Rabbi said, "What is it that has four legs when it's lying down, three legs when it's standing up, and two legs when it's seated?"

The priest said, "Come again?"

The Rabbi said, "What is it that has four legs when it's lying down, three legs when it's standing up, and two legs when it's seated?"

The priest puzzled and puzzled, and finally said to the Rabbi, "I'm afraid I can't answer that one. That really stops me. Here's your $10." Then he asked, "By the way, Rabbi, what is it that has four legs when it's lying down, three legs when it's standing up, and two legs when it's seated?"

The Rabbi said, "I don't know, either, so here's your $1."

45

A man was sitting at a bar, and the bartender and he were watching television. On the screen it showed a man teetering on the edge of the roof of a tall building. It wasn't clear whether he was going to jump or not, and the patron said to the bartender, "I'll bet you $10 he doesn't jump."

The bartender said, "All right, if you want, I'll bet you $10."

So they bet the $10, they watched, and in a couple of minutes, sure enough, the man jumped off the roof. The bartender said to the patron, "Look, I can't take your money. I knew he was going to jump, because I saw it on the 6 o'clock news."

The patron said, "I saw it on the 6 o'clock news also, but I didn't think anyone was stupid enough to do it twice."

46

In Palm Beach, a group was sitting at dinner. There was a fairly attractive-looking man, not young, who sat across from a widow. The widow looked at him and looked at him and looked at him, and finally said, "You know, you look like my fourth husband." He said, "Really? How many times have you been married?" She said, "Three."

47

A widow got married, and after six months she went to see her lawyer and said, "I've got to get a divorce. The man I married is a sex maniac. He doesn't leave me alone, and in the six months that we've been married, I've lost 60 pounds. I must get a divorce."

The lawyer said, "All right. We'll start proceedings, and we'll see. I think you will be able to get it."

As she was leaving, she suddenly turned around and said to him, "Don't start the proceedings for one month. I've got to lose ten more pounds."

48

This is a story of an etymologist...not an entomologist. An entomologist studies bugs. An etymologist studies the source and derivation of words and phrases. And a friend of mine, who is a professor at Columbia, a rather well-known etymologist, decided that he would discover the source of the phrase, "What are you, some kind of nut or something?"

After two years of research, he discovered that the first time the phrase had been used was during the Revolutionary War, when Washington was defeated in the Battle of New York. The troops that had escaped marched south, through New Jersey, and they marched and marched, and after they had gone, oh, over 100 miles, they came to a small town and they stopped at a farmhouse. General Washington's adjutant went to the door and knocked on the door. The farmer's wife came out, and the adjutant said, "I'm General Washington's adjutant and I have a group of men here. We have marched a long distance. Can you possibly take care of us tonight?" ▶

She said, "Well, you're much too large a group for me, but if you look down the road there," she pointed out, "there's a large house and if you go there, I think they ought to be able to take care of you." She said, "If you want to leave one man here, you can. He'll join you in the morning."

The adjutant said, "Thank you, Madam," and turned around and said, "Private Cox, you stay here tonight, and meet us at 6 o'clock in the morning, in front of the house you see down the road there." Private Cox went into the house and they marched down to the other building. Well, the farmer's wife had neglected to tell him that this was a house of ill repute, a house of prostitution. The adjutant knocked on the door. The Madam came to the door.

The adjutant said, "Madam, we are a group of men. We have marched here. Can you possibly take care of all of us tonight?" She said, "How many men are you?" He said, "Ninety-nine, without Cox."

Astonished, she said, "What are you, some kind of nut or something?"

49

There was a newlyappointed college president who came into the office of his retiring predecessor who congratulated him and said to him, "I want to help you and I have left you two envelopes for possible crises during your service as president—Envelope #1 and Envelope #2." He said, "Envelope #1 is to be opened in the event of a student uprising."

There was a student uprising and the new president opened the first envelope and it said, "Blame everything on your predecessor."

Envelope #2 he was instructed to open in the event of a faculty uprising. There was a faculty uprising. He opened the second envelope and it said, "Prepare two envelopes."

50

A man's wife became very ill, and she looked so seriously ill that he called the doctor and convinced him that he should come and visit his wife. The doctor came in with his black bag, took a quick look at the wife, and told the husband to wait outside. The doctor was in with the wife for about 15 minutes, and he came out and said to the husband, "Have you got a hammer?"

The husband said, "Yes," and he got the hammer and gave it to the doctor who went back into the room with the wife.

Another 15 minutes passed, and the doctor came out and he said, "Have you got a screwdriver?"

The husband was puzzled, but he went and got the screwdriver, and gave it to the doctor, who went back into the room.

Another 15 minutes passed and the doctor came out and said to the husband, "Have you got a saw?"

The husband said to the doctor, "I have a saw, Doctor, but I don't understand. Haven't you diagnosed her condition yet?"

The doctor said, "Not yet. I can't get my bag open."

51

Jake Cohen attended a fund-raising dinner for the United Jewish Appeal. There was a strong plea to increase gifts, because of the increased costs of operations. Everyone was moved. Finally, Jake Cohen raised his hand and said, "I gave $50,000 last year."

The man calling the pledge cards said, "I know you did, but we had trouble with you. We had to sue you."

"Well," Jake Cohen said, "this year I'm going to increase my gift. I'm going to give you the $50,000 and I'm going to give you the costs and attorneys' fees also."

52

A friend of mine was in Paris. He was walking along the Rue Faubourg St. Honore, passing various art galleries, and in the window of one he saw a Chagall painting. The painting had a cow on the left side, with a halo over its head. On the right side was a big red tomato and on top of it was a beautiful little donkey. It attracted him and he went in and he spoke to the owner and he said, "You know, I like that Chagall in the window, but I don't understand it. What does it mean—this cow with a halo and the big red tomato with a beautiful donkey on top?" The proprietor said, "It happens that Monsieur Chagall is here with my partner. Why don't you ask him about it?" My friend went over, was introduced to Chagall and asked him the same question. He said, "You know, I like the color and balance of your painting, but I don't understand it. What does it mean, this cow with a halo over its head, and the big red tomato with a beautiful donkey on top?" Chagall said, "That's a beach scene." My friend said, "A beach scene? I don't understand it." "Oh, yes," said Chagall, "I was on the beach with a friend of mine and the most beautiful girl I have ever seen, with the most beautiful figure I have ever seen in my life, and the smallest bikini I have ever seen, came marching past us as we sat on the sand. My friend looked at her and said, "Holy cow! What an ass on that tomato!"

53

A patient came to a psychiatrist and he said, "Doctor, I have two questions I wish you would answer for me."

The doctor said, "What are they?"

The patient said, "The first question is, 'Can a man fall in love with an elephant?'"

The psychiatrist said, "No, it's impossible for a man to fall in love with an elephant. And what's your second question?"

The patient said, "Do you know anyone who would like to buy a very large engagement ring?"

54

There are many English clubs that are limited to male membership. Very few of them allow women in the club at any time. In one particular club, the Board of Governors decided that the members could bring their wives to lunch on Tuesdays. One of the members, who was single, objected and said to the Chairman of the House Committee, "I'm not married, but I do have a mistress. Can I bring my mistress to lunch on Tuesdays?" The Chairman of the House Committee said he would have to review it with the Board of Governors and would let him know. Some time later, he got back to the member and he said, "The Board of Governors has reviewed your problem. They have decided that you can bring your mistress to lunch at the club on Tuesdays, provided that she is the wife of one of the members."

55

In conversation with a friend, a man said that he had lost two wives, and had become a widower twice. His friend said, "How did it happen?"

"Well," he said, "the first wife died from eating poisoned mushrooms."

His friend said, "What about the second wife?"

He said, "The second wife died from a fractured skull."

The friend said, "How did that happen?"

The man said, "She wouldn't eat the mushrooms."

56

A ceremony was being held in Israel at the Tomb of the Unknown Soldier. One man said to the chap standing next to him, "You know, that's Meyer Perlmutter in there, and if you look at the tablet, you'll see that."

The man standing next to him said, "I don't understand. This is the Tomb of the Unknown Soldier. If they knew who it was, why is he there?"

The first man said, "Well, as a soldier, Meyer Perlmutter was unknown. As a furrier, he'll live forever."

57

This is not a funny story, but it is a significant one.

A man once said, "Wouldn't it be a wonderful thing if every day of our lives we had $86,400 in the bank, although we had to spend it entirely each day—we couldn't carry any of it over to the following day." The fact is that each of us has a bank of 86,400 seconds each day of our lives and we can spend those seconds in any way we wish, but we can't carry any of them over to the following day.

This is used in a tribute to someone, of whom you say that he has used his bank of 86,400 seconds for the benefit of mankind, in a way which must generate admiration and praise from all his contemporaries.

58

A man was playing golf on a course with very severe roughs beside the fairway and he sliced a ball far into the rough. He started to go in to look for it and the caddie said to him, "You better take a club with you when you look for the ball."

The man said, "How can I pick a club until I see the ball and the kind of lie I have?"

The caddie said, "Take any club, it's not for the ball, it's for the snakes."

59

A man came into a supermarket, went up to the counter, and said to the clerk behind, "I want a half of that chicken in the counter there."

The clerk said, "We don't sell half chickens. We have chicken parts. You can buy them."

The man said, "No, I don't want chicken parts. I want half of that chicken."

The clerk said, "I told you, we don't sell it that way."

The man said, "I insist. I'm a good customer and if you want, you can talk to the manager. I insist, I want a half of that chicken."

The clerk moved down along the counter, came to the manager, and said, "Look, there's some crazy guy wants me to give him half of that chicken"—and then he turned around and noticed that the man had followed him and heard what he was saying. So he said to the manager, "And this gentleman wants to buy the other half."

So he sold him the half chicken. ▶

The manager said to the clerk, "You know, that was very quick-witted of you."

He said, "Maybe you are qualified for a better job in our organization. Where do you come from?"

He said, "I come from Canada."

"Really," the manager said, "why did you leave Canada?"

"Well," he said, "in Canada there are only hockey players and whores."

The manager said, "Is that so? It happens that my wife comes from Canada."

The clerk said, "Is that so. Tell me, what team did she play on?"

60

I had occasion to be in Chicago to speak at a dinner, and I had arranged with my wife to meet me at a plane which arrived at 12:30 in the morning. I missed the plane. The next plane wasn't due for three hours. My wife, when I didn't appear, and when she learned that there was no plane for three hours, figured that I must have stayed with somebody if the dinner took longer than I expected. So she sent a wire to each of my five best friends in Chicago and asked whether I was spending the night with them. In the meantime, I took the plane three hours later and I got a taxi and got home about four hours later than I was expected. In the morning, my wife received five telegrams. Each of my friends said yes, that I was spending the night with him.

61

The Harmonie Club in New York for many years restricted its membership to Jewish citizens of German descent. An applicant appeared before the Admissions Committee and was asked whether his parents came from Russia. He said no. He was taken in as a member. Some time later, he was called before the Board of Governors and charged with having lied to the Admissions Committee. He said, "How?"

They said, "When you were asked whether your parents came from Russia, you said no."

"Well," he said, "I didn't lie. They're still there."

62

A friend of mine was recommended to a psychiatrist at Fifth Avenue and 71st Street. He went into the psychiatrist's office and was told by the girl at the desk to go into the next room and he would see signs indicating where he should go. He went into the next room and saw two doors. Over one door, it said, "Men." Over the other it said, "Women." He went through the door marked "Men" and he came into a room and there were two doors and one door said, "Men over 45 Years of Age." The other door said, "Men under 45 Years of Age," so he went through the first door and he came into a room and there were two doors. One door said, "Men with Incomes over $80,000 a Year" and the other said, "Men with Incomes under $80,000 a Year." Well, he was a very wealthy man. His income was far in excess of $80,000 a year, but he wasn't going to tell the doctor that. So he went through the door marked, "Men with Incomes under $80,000 a Year," and he found himself out on Fifth Avenue and 71st Street.

63

Mr. and Mrs. Goldberg were lying in bed and the window was open somewhat and she said, "Jake, please close the window. It's cold outside."

Jake said, "So if I close the window, it will be warm outside?"

64

This is the story of three amateur Jewish philosophers who were sitting in Ratner's and were drinking glasses of tea. The first one said, "You know, when I die, I would like to lie next to Chaim Weizmann. He was a great man and really more responsible for the founding of Israel than anybody else."

The second man said, "I would like to lie next to Louis Brandeis. He was a great judge and one of the greatest American Jews that ever lived."

. The third man said, "I would like to lie next to Raquel Welch."

His friend said, "But she's not dead yet." He said, "Neither am I."

65

This story relates to the war that began in Israel in 1967 between the Arabs and the Jews. There were two people who lived in Tel Aviv, an Arab and a Jew, who were neighbors for many years and who were very fond of each other. Each one had a dog. The Arab, who had a big German police dog, said to his friend the Jew, "Look, there's no reason for us to fight." He said, "You have a dog. I have a dog. Let the two dogs fight and let them decide who is the winner."

The Jew, who had a little motley-looking animal, said, "All right." So the two dogs were put in a ring together and they fought, and this little mixed-up creature tore the big German Shepherd apart.

Finally, when it was over, the Arab said to the Jew, "You know, I am amazed." He said, "I never saw a dog like yours. Tell me, what kind of breed is he?"

The Jew said, "Well, it's a little difficult to tell, but before he had his nose fixed, he was a crocodile."

66

A lady came into a delicatessen and said to the man behind the counter, "I'd like to have a turkey sandwich."

He said, "I'm sorry, lady, I don't have any turkey."

She said, "All right, I'll take a chicken sandwich."

The owner behind the counter said, "Lady, if I had chicken, wouldn't I give you a turkey sandwich?"

67

This is the story of this nice young Jewish man who was close to his mother and came to see her every Friday night. She sent him a birthday gift of two ties. The next Friday night when he came to her house, he wore one of the ties. When he came in, his mother said, ''What's the matter, you don't like the other tie?''

68

Abe Cohen liked scuba-diving. He had his outfit on. He was down in the water, near the bottom, and all of a sudden he saw his friend Jake Schwartz come floating down with no equipment on, and no helmet—no nothing. So he said to him, "Jake, for God's sake, what are you doing down here?"

Jake said, "What am I doing?—I'm drowning."

69

Judge Proskauer, a former judge and a very well-known lawyer in New York City, had a testimonial dinner on the occasion of his 90th birthday. Everybody who got up said that he was such a wonderful man, so capable and so friendly to everybody. Everyone spoke very favorably about him. Finally, when he was about to be introduced, one of the men there said, "You know, Judge Proskauer, it's amazing. You were a trial lawyer, you had adversaries in most of the things you handled, and yet everyone who speaks of you speaks of you so favorably and compliments you on your generosity and your kindness." He said, "How is it possible that you could live to be 90 and conduct that kind of a legal practice and not have any enemies?"

Judge Proskauer said, "Easy. I outlived the bastards."

70

Mr. Ginsberg traveled to Europe for the first time on the Queen Elizabeth. He was alone and he was seated by the purser with a Frenchman. When Mr. Ginsberg came to the first meal, the Frenchman stood up and said, "Bon appetit." Mr. Ginsberg didn't know what it meant, but he thought the Frenchman was telling him his name. He said, "Ginsberg." The second meal, the same thing happened. The Frenchman said, "Bon appetit," and Ginsberg said, "Ginsberg." After the third meal, Ginsberg went to the purser and said, "I don't understand this guy you sat me with. Every time I sit down to eat with him, he tells me his name." The purser said, "What does he say?" Ginsberg said, "Bon appetit." The purser said, "He's not telling you his name, he is wishing you a good appetite—that you will enjoy your meal." "Oh," Ginsberg said, "I'm sorry. I didn't understand it." So the following meal, before the Frenchman even had a chance to open his mouth, Ginsberg jumped up and said, "Bon appetit." The Frenchman replied, "Ginsberg."

71

A friend of mine was told that he was very ill and that he had six months to live. "Well," he said, "if that's true, I think I'll become a Communist."

He was asked why. He said, "Better one of them should die, than one of us."

72

This is the story of a dress manufacturer who was unable to sell a good part of his line, the normal price for which was $39.75 a dress. The dresses were hanging on the racks and he was getting sicker and sicker as he saw them and he finally called in the sales manager and said, "Look, I can't stand looking at these. Take these dresses to Gimbel's and offer them to Gimbel's for $15 apiece. They can clean out the whole thing." The sales manager went to Gimbel's and he came back and told the owner that Gimbel's wouldn't take them.

The dresses hung on the racks for a couple of more weeks and finally the owner said to the sales manager, "I'm going to die if I continue to look at these." He said, "Go to Macy's and give them to Macy's for $10 apiece. The sales manager went to Macy's and came back and said they wouldn't take them. A couple of more weeks went by and finally the owner said, "Look, take all the dresses up to Loehmann's and let them have them at $5 apiece. I can't look at them anymore." The sales manager went to Loehmann's, but came back soon, saying that Loehmann's wouldn't take them. ►

After several weeks, the owner says to the sales manager, "I'm going to drop dead if I have to look at these things. Take them down to the UJA and give them to the UJA for nothing." The sales manager came back and said to the owner, "I took them to the UJA, but they said they are sorry, they can't take them—their Fall line is complete. When you make your Spring line, they will be glad to deal with you."

73

There was a professor at Brandeis University named Claude Vigee, who taught French. He had a leave of absence and at a meeting of the Board of Trustees it was reported by the Chairman of the Academic Committee that Claude Vigee asked for an additonal six months' leave, to finish a book. At that particular moment, one of the Trustees, who shall be nameless, awoke from the nap that he usually took during the meeting of the Board. He said, "What was that?" The Chairman said that Professor Claude Vigee has asked for an extension of his six months' leave of absence, to finish a book. The Trustee said, "Is that so? What book is he reading?"

74

A Pope died and went to heaven. St. Peter gave him a modest size house, with a nice little garden and he was reasonably content, except that next to him was a beautiful large house with magnificent grounds. The Pope went to St. Peter and said, "St. Peter, I don't understand it." He said, "I was a Pope on earth and that's very important, and," he said, "next to me is this beautiful big house with lovely grounds, and I am wondering who occupies it?"

St. Peter said, "It's occupied by a lawyer."

The Pope said, "A lawyer? I don't understand. After all," he said, "a Pope is a most important person on earth.

St. Peter said, "Here in heaven, we have a lot of Popes, but we have only one lawyer."

75

A man came to a motel in New Hampshire in the dead of winter. There was a terrible snowstorm going on outside, and he came in and said to the clerk, "I've got to have a room," and the clerk said, "You're very lucky. I just got a cancellation over the phone, because of the ,storm. It's the last room I have, you can have it." He started to walk away and a very beautiful girl came up behind him and said to the clerk, "I'm going to die out there. I can't move my car, the snow is so high, and it's terrible and I'm freezing, it's so cold. Have you got a room for me?" The clerk said to her, "You heard what I said to the gentleman just going down there. I don't have anything else." So the girl ran after the man. She said, "Look, sir, you know I don't know you, and you don't know me, and we don't know them and they don't know us, and there are two beds in your room. It wouldn't hurt you and it would really save my life, if you would let me sleep in one of the beds and you can sleep in the other bed. If I have to go outside, I'm going to die." ▶

He was moved and he said, "All right." So they both went into the room and each one undressed and got into bed. And, after a while, the girl said to the man, "You know, I'm still very cold." She said, "I don't know you, you don't know me, we don't know them, and they don't know us. If I were to come into your bed, both of us would be much warmer. May I come?" He said, "All right." So they were there for a while and proximity brought ideas and she said to the man, "You know, I don't know you and you don't know me, we don't know them and they don't know us. How about a party?" He said, "If I don't know you and you don't know me and we don't know them, and they don't know us, whom are we going to invite to the party?"

76

The poor Arab was crawling along the ground in the desert calling, "Water, water, please give me water." A Jew walked by and he was carrying a sample case of ties. "You know, I got some beautiful ties here," he said to the Arab. "They are selling for only $15 apiece. You want some ties?" The Arab said, "Water, water, please give me some water." The Jew said, "Look, I'll make a special deal for you. You can have a tie for $10 if you want." The Arab said, "All I want is water, water. I must have water." The Jew said, "This is my final offer—You can have one or more ties for $5 apiece, but that's the lowest I'll sell them for." The Arab said, "Give me water, water, please." The Jew said, "Ach—you won't buy them. You go five miles down—there is an oasis. My brother is there. He has a restaurant. You go to the restaurant and he'll give you some water." So the Arab crawled along the ground for five miles still calling for water, and he came to the oasis and he came to the restaurant. He crawled to the door of the restaurant and the proprietor, the brother of the tie salesman, was there and the Arab said, "Water, water, please give me some water."

The proprietor said, "Go away. You can't come in here without a tie."

77

The young Jewish mother had named her son Stetson. After a while, one of her friends said to her, "How did you happen to select a name like Stetson?" She said, "Well, I'll tell you what happened. We expected a girl. We had a name for the girl, but we didn't expect a boy. But at the briss we had so many friends and everybody was telling me that the name should be this, the name should be that, and I decided I would leave it to fate. So," she said, "I asked everybody to write the name he suggested or she suggested on a piece of paper and we put them all in a hat and after they were all in the hat, we mixed them all up and I reached down and my hands got hold of one piece of paper and it was a little sticky, but it came out and on the piece of paper it said, 'Stetson!'"

78

There was a convent where the nuns lived in poverty and their physical accommodations were primitive. Finally, someone made a gift and instead of using chamber pots in the various bedrooms, they were able to put in central plumbing. The Mother Superior, who was very frugal, decided that they shouldn't just throw away the chamber pots. So she got one of the Sisters to put all the chamber pots on a truck and go down to the Waste Management Corporation, to see whether or not they could realize any money for the chamber pots. As she was driving along in the truck that the convent owned, it suddenly ran out of gas. The Sister got out, remembering that she had passed a gas station about a mile back. She took one of the chamber pots, went back to the gas station, filled it with gasoline and walked back to the truck. She took off the cap of the gas tank and, as she was pouring in the gasoline from the chamber pot, a truck came by with a nice Irish driver. He looked over to her and said, "Sister, that's what I call faith!"

79

The Catholic was told by his doctor that he had six months to live. He changed his whole way of life. He started to go to Mass three times a day. He helped people, made gifts, did everything possible to try to make sure that he would be accepted into heaven.

The Protestant was told that he had six months to live. He changed his Will and he also changed his attitude toward other people and was generous and kind.

The Jew was told that he had six months to live, and he changed his doctor.

80

Just before the performance at the theater began, a man in the fourth row stood up and said, "Is there a Christian Scientist in the house? Is there a Christian Scientist in the house?" A man in the back stood up and said, "I'm a Christian Scientist." The first man said, "Will you please change seats with me? I'm in a draft."

81

The president and the executive director of the United Fund were traveling together through Europe, when they came to Rome. They saw the Coliseum from the window of their hotel and the president said to the executive director, "You see what happens to a building project if you don't have the money beforehand."

82

Rose and Joseph Shapiro had died in an automobile accident and were sitting on Cloud 9, sailing along up in heaven. In front of Cloud 9 there was Cloud 8 which was moving at a very, very slow rate and behind Cloud 9 were Cloud 10 and other clouds. Joseph decided to pass Cloud 8, so he put his hand out and started to go around the cloud in front of him. His wife said to him, "Now you put your hand out."

83

Mr. Ginsberg and his secretary were engaged in a little extra-curricular activity in bed when she said to him, "The window is open and it's very, very cold." Mr. Ginsberg said, "Would you like to make like Mrs. Ginsberg?" The secretary said, "Yes." And he said to her, "Then you close the window."

84

A definition of nursing—It is said that a good nurse can make a bed without disturbing the patient. A doctor friend of mine said that an excellent nurse is one who can make the patient without disturbing the bed.

85

This is really advice to the mother of children who go to camp. Young boys neglect to write to their parents and a friend of mine has developed a system which is infallible. She knows how to make her son write. What she does is, she writes to him at camp and says she is enclosing $5 so that he can buy anything that he wants. Her friend said to her, "I don't understand. How does that get him to write?" "Well," she said, "of course you forget to enclose the $5."

86

A Jew who had decided to convert to Catholicism, was put through a test and asked various questions after he had studied for it. He was asked, "Where was Jesus born?" He thought for a while and he said, "Pittsburgh?" They said no. He said "Allentown?" They said no. He said, "Where was it?" They said, "Bethlehem." he said, "Was I so far away?"

87

This is the story of a man who loved herring. On Broadway, in the 80s, was a famous restaurant known as Steinbergs, which dealt in milk products and where you could get the best herring possible, and he used to go there. And one day he goes in and he orders a plate of herring. They serve it to him and he pushes aside the sour cream and the onions and, there on the plate, he sees a herring with crossed eyes. The crossed eyes upset him so much he couldn't eat and he went away and for two weeks he couldn't look at a herring. But the desire returned and he went back to Steinbergs, and again he ordered a herring, and they served him a herring and there on the plate, after he pushed aside the sour cream and the onions, was the same cross-eyed herring. This time he was so upset, that he went away and for a solid month he didn't eat herring. He decided that this time, instead of going back to Steinbergs, he would go to Lindy's and he ordered herring. They brought him a beautiful plate of herring covered with onions and sour cream, with some wonderful pumpernickel bread on the side. He rubbed his hands together, pushing aside the sour cream and the onions—but still, there on the plate lay the same cross-eyed herring. And the herring looked up at him saying "Aha! So you don't eat at Steinberg's anymore."

88

This is the story of the husband who was criticising his wife because she drew checks on the account beyond the amount of the balance, and he said that she was constantly overdrawn.

She answered him—"I'm not overdrawn. You're just underdeposited."

89

This is the story of the man who was very regular in his habits. At 8:26 every morning, he went to the john and evacuated. On one occasion, he got an infection. Some germs got into his system. He went to the doctor and the doctor told him that he would have to take cortisone. Well, the three germs in his system heard this. The first germ said, "Look, cortisone is going to hurt us. I'm going to the very end of his big toe and maybe it won't reach me." The second germ said, "I'm going to the very tip of his little finger and maybe the cortisone won't reach me there." The third germ said, "I'm going out on the 8:26."

90

This is the story of a 103-year-old lady who actually was interviewed on television and she said she had a peculiar experience. She went on a bus and was standing in front of a very old man who was sitting down, and the old man said to her, "You know, I'm very old. If I weren't, I would get up and give you my seat, but I tell you, if you feel tired, you can sit down on my lap."

Well, she felt tired, so she sat down on his lap and after a few minutes, he said to her, "Look, my dear, you had better stand up. I'm not as old as I thought I was."

91

A Polish man was trained by the new political group in Poland, who had decided that they were going to prove to the world that Polish men were intelligent. They were going to kill the concept of Poles being stupid. So they trained men in different languages and they trained one to go to America and speak English and they carefully trained him to go to the store and say, "I want a roast beef sandwich and a Coca-Cola."

Well, he came to New York City, he went to the store, and he said very carefully, "I want a roast beef sandwich and a Coca-Cola."

The clerk said, "You must be Polish," and the first man said, "Yes, I am, but how did you possibly know?"

The clerk said, "This is a hardware store."

92

This Irish chap fell very ill and was taken to the Catholic hospital, where he incurred tremendous medical expenses. The Sister in charge of the financial office of the hospital came to him and said, "Do you have any Medicare or Medicaid?"

He said, "No."

"Do you have any money?"

"No."

"Do you have any relatives who can help you with your hospital bills?"

He said, "I have only one relative and she's not married. She's a nun."

"Oh, you mustn't say that," the Sister said, "You should know that when your sister became a nun, she married our Lord."

"In that case," he said, "Send the bill to my brother-in-law."

93

Two ladies were discussing their experiences in moving picture theaters. Said one to the other, "I went there alone and it was terrible. I had to move my seat five times."

The other said, "Were you molested?"

The answer—"Yes, finally."

100 STORIES

Section II

The following stories may not be appropriate for all mixed company. They might be called my locker-room stories. You must decide if you should tell them and where.

94

The Columbia professor was driving downtown and stopped at a red light. A panhandler came over and said, "Hey, Bud, will you lend me $2 for something to eat and drink?"

"Neither a lender nor a borrower be—William Shakespeare," said the professor.

"F--k you—Tennessee Williams."," retorted the angry panhandler.

95

The girls were tired of Alice's artistic pretensions. She knew everything about art, and every artist. So the girls cooked up something.

When Alice returned from a visit to Paris, they asked if she had been to the art galleries. "Oh, yes," she said. "I was in every art dealer's shop and saw everything—Impressionists, Post-Impressionists, Moderns, classic painters. The prices are outrageous."

"You did see the modern painters?"

"Oh yes. Every one of them."

"Did you see any paintings by Tihsolluf?"

"Yes I did. I didn't like them much—and the prices were much too high."

The girls all giggled. Tihsolluf was "Full o' Shit" backwards.

96

During World War II, General Patton, who was a stickler for compliance with military regulations and rules, appeared at the camp of a military unit known as the Rangers. At three o'clock one morning when the temperature was 5⁰ outside—it was in France—he ordered that the men were to be lined up for dress parade. Finally, all stood there. You probably remember that General Patton normally carried a riding crop. He walked along the row of men and came to one who had three buttons open in his shirt. So he smacked him across the chest with the riding crop, as hard as he could, and said, "Did that hurt you?"

The soldier said, "No." ▶

The General said, "Why not?" The soldier said, "Because I'm a Ranger and the Rangers are the greatest military outfit in the United States Army."

Patton went farther along and one of the men there had a rather dirty face. He needed a shave very badly and General Patton took his riding crop and smacked him across the face. He said to the man, "Does that hurt you?"

The soldier said, "No."

The General said "Why not?"

He said, "Because we Rangers are accustomed to experiencing and withstanding pain, and the Rangers are the best outfit in the world."

General Patton went a little further and he came to one man whose male organ was sticking way out. General Patton took his riding crop and smacked it across the male organ, as hard as he could, and he said to the man, "Does that hurt you?"

The man said, "No."

The General said, "Why not?" and the man said, "Because it belongs to the man behind me."

97

Mr. Goldberg came home with a black eye. He had been at temple that morning. Mrs. Goldberg said, "What happened to you?"

"Well," he said, "you know Mrs. Shapiro sits in front of me, and, you know, you get up and you sit down, and you get up and you sit down in the service, and I noticed that when she got up her dress was caught between the cheeks of her rear end. Because I was sure she wouldn't like that, I reached over and pulled it out, and she turned around and smacked me in my eye."

His wife said, "Well, I don't blame her."

The following week he came back after temple again and the other eye was blackened and his wife said, "For God's sake, what happened?"

He said, "Well, I told you about Mrs. Shapiro. Well, this week we were in temple and the same thing happened. She got up and sat down and got up and sat down, and again her dress was caught between her cheeks and Mr. Cohen, who was standing next to me, reached over and pulled it out, and I said to him 'Mr. Cohen, Mrs. Shapiro doesn't like that. She likes it in,' and I pushed it back in and she swung around and hit me in the other eye."

98

A man came into a bar and sat down. He had a paper bag with him and he reached in and took out a small piano that he put on the bar. He reached in again and put a small stool in front of the piano. Then he reached in and he brought up a little 12-inch man, who sat down at the piano and started to play.

The bartender said, "I never saw anything like this in my life. Tell me, where in God's name did you ever get anything like that?"

The patron said, "Look, you may not believe me, but during the war I was stranded on a deserted island, and," he said, "after a few days, a bottle was washed up on shore and it was corked and I pulled out the cork and out came a genie.

"And the genie said, 'You have saved my life and you may have one wish. Any wish that you want will be granted.'

"And," the patron said, "the genie misunderstood me. He thought I said I wanted a 12-inch pianist."

99

A man came to Andrew Mellon and said, "I'll bet you $10,000 that you have three testicles." Andrew Mellon said, "That's crazy." "Oh, no," the man said, "I'm serious. I want to bet you $10,000. I'll deposit it with you right now, and you can hold it. I'll be back in a week and we'll see." Andrew Mellon said, "Well, if you insist on throwing away $10,000, I won't argue with you." So he took the $10,000.

The man came back a week later with another chap, and he said to Mr. Mellon, "Now let me see whether or not you do have three testicles." Andrew Mellon let down his pants, and the second man fell to the floor in a dead faint. Andrew Mellon said to the first man, "I don't understand. What's the matter with your friend?" "Well," he said, "there's nothing the matter with him, it just happens that I bet him $50,000 that I could get you to take your pants down."

100

This is a story of two nurses in a well-known hospital in New York. One nurse was very beautiful and very attractive. The other nurse was quite ugly. The ugly nurse came to the nurses' desk and said to her beautiful friend, "You know, I have the strangest patient in Room 301. He is tattooed over every inch of his body."

The beautiful nurse said, "Every inch of his body?"

The ugly nurse said, "Yes, absolutely. Every inch of his body."

The beautiful one said, "What about his male organ?"

The ugly nurse said, "He is tattooed there too. He has the word 'tiny' tattooed right there and I saw it."

She said, "If you don't believe it, go in and look at it yourself."

The beautiful nurse said, "I think I will," and she went in and she came out an hour later. The ugly nurse said to her, "Wasn't he tattooed all over his body, as I told you?"

The beautiful nurse said, "He certainly was. But," she said, "on his male organ, he didn't have 'tiny', he had 'Ticonderoga, New York.'"

Section III

If you have been a good girl or a good boy and have read all the 100 Stories and plan to use at least some of them, you can enjoy the following bonus of five additional stories.

Bonus 1

A friend of mine who is 86 years of age went to his doctor and told him that he was getting married. The doctor said, "At 86, how long can it last? Tell me, how old was your father when he died?" My friend answered, "Did I say my father died?" The doctor said, "He's still living? How old is he?" My friend said, "104." The doctor said, "That's wonderful. All right," he said, "How old was your grandfather when he died?" My friend said, "Did I say my grandfather died?" The doctor said, "That's amazing. How old is he?" My friend answered, "122, and not only that, he is getting married." The doctor said, "Why would a man of 122 want to get married?" My friend said, "Did I say he *wanted* to get married?"

Bonus 2

Father Murphy, Pastor Robinson, and Rabbi Rapaport were good friends and were discussing "when life began." Father Murphy said that life began at the moment of conception. Pastor Robinson said life began when the child was born. Rabbi Rapaport said, "When the children get married and the dog dies, life begins."

Bonus 3

The two Salvation Army girls had just finished their out-door stint. It was a warm day and they were taking a shower. One girl looked at the other and said, "You know, you have the largest navel I have ever seen in my life." The other one said, "Is that so? From now on, I'll beat the drum and you'll carry the flag."

Bonus 4

Father Murphy, Pastor Robinson and Rabbi Rapaport were discussing sex. The question arose as to whether it was easy or difficult for the women. Father Murphy said he had no experience in that area and really could not pass an opinion. Pastor Robinson said that he and his wife were not very aggressive people and had never made a study of the subject and his wife was very modest and never told him. Rabbi Rapaport said he was convinced that it was easy, because, he said, if it were difficult, his wife would have the maid do it.

Bonus 5

Father Timothy Healy is the president of Georgetown University. For many years he tried to have women undergraduates at the college. After a long struggle he succeeded, and the undergraduate student body was made co-educational. The question then arose as to where the dormitories for the women should be built. Father Healy looked out the window and pointed to the cemetery of this Jesuit institution. "Right on top of that cemetery," he said. He was asked why and he answered, "Because the ones buried there were the ones who told me that women could come here only over their dead bodies."